MW01152978

better together*

*This book is best read together, grownup and kid.

a kids
book
about

a kids book about

GAY PARENTS

by Jonathan & Thomas West

a
kids
book
about

Text and design copyright © 2023
by A Kids Book About, Inc.

Copyright is good! It ensures that work like this can exist, and more work in the future can be created.

All rights reserved. No part of this publication may be reproduced, distributed, or transmitted in any form or by any means, including photocopying, recording, other electronic or mechanical methods, without the prior written permission of the publisher, except in the case of brief quotations embodied in critical reviews and certain other noncommercial uses permitted by copyright law. For permission requests, write to the publisher.

A Kids Book About, Kids Are Ready, and the colophon 'a' are trademarks of A Kids Book About, Inc.

Printed in the United States of America.

A Kids Book About books are available online: *akidsco.com*

To share your stories, ask questions, or inquire about bulk purchases (schools, libraries, and nonprofits), please use the following email address: *hello@akidsco.com*

Print ISBN: 978-1-958825-35-8
Ebook ISBN: 978-1-958825-36-5

Designed by Rick DeLucco
Edited by Emma Wolf

For Grace, Charlotte, Eleanor, and Henry.

You are loved, you are wanted,
and you will always belong.

Intro

How many gay parents do you know? Probably not many, but that's OK. That's why we wrote this book!

Most of us already know that families can look different, but how often do we think about the different types of parents in our communities? We're 2 dads with 4 kids and want to help you teach the kids in your life that there's no right or wrong way to be a family.

We hope that sharing our family's story will help build greater compassion and understanding for gay parents and their kids. Our story shows others they are not alone and can be proud of who they are.

This book is designed to help people learn that the kids of gay parents are loved, wanted, and they belong, and to teach them that families are built on love, no matter who their parents are.

This book is about

FAMI

ILIES.

In our family, there are 2 dads.

Our kids call us

DADDY and **PAPA.**

We even have hats we like
to wear that say that!

Other grownups call us
Jonathan and Thomas.

When we met a very very long time ago, we knew we loved each other.

But, it wasn't until we saw our friends starting families that we knew being a family was what we wanted.

We knew creating a family was important, amazing, and the right path forward for us.

So right away, we began.

Together, we started calling people to learn more about adoption.

And we did
LOTS and LOTS
of homework.

Although we built our family through adoption, we've found there are many ways to build a family:

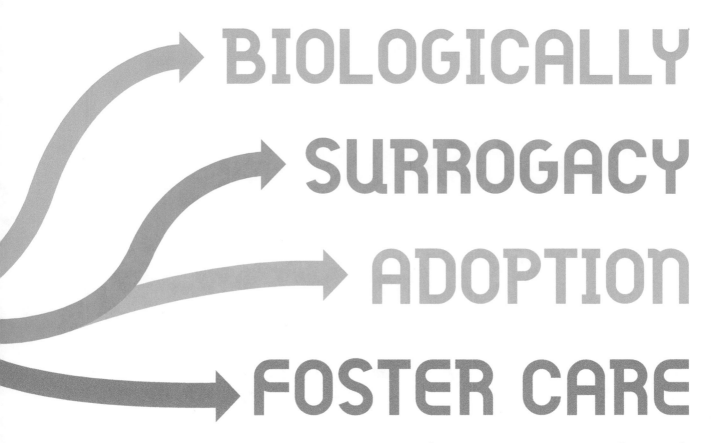

BIOLOGICALLY

SURROGACY

ADOPTION

FOSTER CARE

(to name a few!)

1 of our kids tells her friends that she has a daddy, a papa, and a birth family.

And another of our kids likes to talk about their first biological family and their second adoptive family.

In our family, it's important that our kids know where they came from.

We build traditions together, and we also work to stay true to our kids' inherited traditions from their birth families.

No matter who we are as a family today, we want our kids to hold on to their own heritage.

When we were growing up, we didn't see people in our communities, on television, or in movies or books who looked like us.

Even though we're grownups now, we didn't know it was possible to have a family, because we hadn't seen one like ours.

Something important to us
is being as visible as we can
to show ourselves, our family,
and EVERYONE that a family
like ours is amazing and possible.

It's something we call...

"ACCEPTANCE THROUGH VISIBILITY."

If we can make a difference for 1 other person or 1 other family, we know we've done the right thing by sharing our story.

And no matter who you grow up to be, you can build a family too.

Families look different,
no matter if you have...

A MOM AND A DAD, 2 MOMS,
2 DADS, 1 MOM, 1 DAD,
A GRANDPARENT RAISING YOU,
DIFFERENT SKIN COLORS,
DIFFERENT HAIR TYPES,
OR DIFFERENT TRADITIONS!

Some people think families should only be a mom, a dad, and kids, but we know that's not true.

There are so many types of families!

Ours is just 1 kind.

We want you to know,

WHATEVER
YOUR FAMILY IS,
IT IS EXACTLY RIGHT
AND NOT BETTER
OR WORSE THAN
ANY OTHER FAMILY.

Right now, our family is 2 dads, 4 kids, 3 dogs, 4 ducks, and 5 chickens.

And people always ask if we plan to grow our family.

Our answer is...

WE DON'T KNOW.

Daddy always says no,
but Papa says maybe.

Our answer together
is we'll know when it's right,
just like we always have.

It took a lot of hard work
to build our family.

There were times we weren't
sure it was going to happen.

And we want you to know that the kids of gay parents are wanted, loved, and they belong.

In our house, we like to be

BE ADVENTUROUS, SILLY,
MOVIES, EAT POPCORN, HA
PLAY ON THE SWINGS, RIDE
WITH REAL MAPLE SYRUP,
READ BOOKS, WEAR LOTS
(BECAUSE WE LIVE IN VER

AND ACCEPTING, WATCH
VE BREAKFAST FOR DINNER,
OUR BIKES, EAT PANCAKES
MAKE MOLASSES COOKIES,
OF PLAID AND SWEATERS
MONT), AND BE NORMAL,

just like your family.*

*In our family, whenever anyone toots (farts!), we say, "Ta-da!"

As 2 dads, we do all the things every other parent does.

We change poopy diapers,

make breakfast and school lunches every morning,

pick out clothes,

brush hair AND teeth,

drop kids off at school,

do lots and lots of laundry,

help with homework,

make dinner,

and eat lots of ice cream together.

All parents have a lifelong responsibility to their kids.

We have chosen them and
brought them into our lives.

We made the choice to care for, love, support, and raise our kids for as long as we're alive.

It's a lot like the promises
we made to one another, out
of love, when we got married.

WE CHOSE
TO BE P

TO DO THIS. ARENTS.

It isn't always easy,
it isn't always fun, but
our family is what
we've chosen.

For all of the times that are hard, there are many more moments which remind us why we chose to start a family in the first place.

Like watching our kids grow,
or the first time our kid said,

"HI, PAPA."

Love truly makes a family.

Our family may look different from yours, or maybe we look the same.

But at the end of the day,

LOVE IS WHAT

UNITES US ALL.

Outro

Now that you've learned more about gay parents and what diversity looks like, it's time to do the hard part. Talk to your kids about any of the preconceived notions you might have about gay parents and their families. Kids are ready to learn and learn best when the grownups in their lives are honest, transparent, and vulnerable.

To start, read this book again together and be honest about how it made you feel. You can even reach out to us on our socials if you find yourself stuck on something.

Next, share this book with your friends and family. They might have some of the same preconceived notions that you had before reading our book. It's never too early (or late) to start this important conversation.

Finally, help us do the work outside of this book. Share our story whenever the topic comes up. Let's change the ill-conceived narrative that all families look 1 way. All kids deserve a home where they are wanted and loved, and we know it doesn't matter who their parents are to achieve that.

About The Author

Jonathan (he/him) and Thomas (he/him) West wrote this book for their 4 adopted children and the kids of other gay parents.

They believe it is essential for all kids and grownups to know that the makeup of families is different for EVERYONE! And just because someone else's family may look different than yours, it is exactly right, not better or worse.

Jonathan and Thomas believe in sharing their story by being visible to others, so everyone can realize the dream of becoming a parent.

They hope to be the change that allows future parents to be authentic and step into parenthood full of pride and love.

 @daddyandpapa   @thedaddyandpapa

 www.daddyandpapa.com   @thedaddyandpapa

a kids book about MONEY
by ... Stramwasser

kids book about BEING INCLUSIVE
by Ashton Mota & Rebekah Bruesehoff

a kids book about diversity
by Charnaie Gordon

kids book about LEADERSHIP
by Orion Jean

kids book about IMMIG...
by MJ Calder...

a kids book about SAFETY

by Soraya Sutherlin, CEM
in partnership with JUDY

a kids book about CLIMATE CHANGE
by Zanagee Artis & Olivia Greenspan

a kids book about IMAGINATION
by LEVAR BURTON

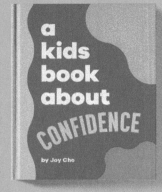
a kids book about CONFIDENCE
by Joy Cho

a kids b a... Se...
by Ev...

kids book about ...XIETY
by ... Szabo
...ind Happy Faces

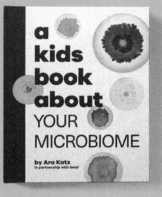
a kids book about YOUR MICROBIOME
by Ara Katz
in partnership with Seed

a kids book about racism
by Jelani Memory

a kids book about DISABILITIES
by Kristine Napper

a kids boo abo bore...
by KYLE St...

a kids book about DIVORCE
by Ashley Simpo

a kids book about cancer
by Dr. Kelsie Storm & Sarah Porter

a kids book about BEING TRANSGENDER
by Gia Parr
in partnership with The GenderCool Project

a kids book about DEPRESSION
by Kileah McIlvain

a ki bo ab...
by Mei...

kids book about ...ame

a kids book about THE TULSA RACE MASSACRE

Discover more at akidsco.com

CPSIA information can be obtained
at www.ICGtesting.com
Printed in the USA
BVHW012002170523
664374BV00001B/1

9 781958 825358